Jasper
Alfred Chen.

Feb 12 98

SHARKS

A PORTRAIT OF THE ANIMAL WORLD

Andrew Cleave

TODTRI

This book was designed and produced by
Todtri Productions Limited
P.O. Box 20058
New York, NY 10023-1482
Fax: (212) 279-1241

Printed and bound in Singapore

ISBN 1-880908-25-5

Producer: Robert M. Tod
Book Designer: Mark Weinberg
Photo Editor: Edward Douglas
Editors: Mary Forsell, Joanna Wissinger, Don Kennison
Production Co-ordinator: Heather Weigel
DTP Associates: Jackie Skroczky, Adam Yellin
Typesetting: Command-O, NYC

PHOTO CREDITS

Photographer/Page Number

Innerspace Visions
Tom Campbell 19 (bottom), 76 (top & bottom)
Mark Conlin 6, 11 (top & bottom), 26, 30 (bottom), 37, 42, 52, 55, 67 (bottom), 68 (top, center & bottom)
David B. Fleetham 5, 30 (top), 38, 69, 70
Howard Hall 22
Nigel Marsh 12 (bottom), 13 (bottom), 16, 17 (top)
Amos Nachoum 56-57
Doug Perrine 10, 12 (top), 15, 19 (top), 21, 27, 31 (bottom), 32, 34 (top & bottom), 50 (top), 54, 59, 64, 66, 71, 74
Bruce Rasner 77 (top)
Carl Roessler 45 (right)
Norine Rouse 67 (top)
Mark Strickland 20 (top), 39, 60 (bottom)
Ron & Valerie Taylor 3, 7, 14 (top), 29, 53, 65
James D. Watt 24-25, 46, 72-73
Norbert Wu 8-9, 11 (center), 31 (top), 50 (bottom)

Ocean Images
Walt Clayton 49

Tom Stack & Associates
Kerry T. Givens 33 (top)
Brian Parker 48
Ed Robinson 14 (bottom)

Marty Snyderman
17 (bottom), 20 (bottom), 23, 28 (top), 35, 36, 43, 44-45, 47, 60 (top), 62, 78

The Waterhouse
Stephen Frink 51, 56 (bottom left), 61
Carl Roessler 75

The Wildlife Collection
Gary Bell 13 (top), 63, 77 (bottom)
John Giustina 33 (bottom)
Richard Hermann 4, 28 (bottom)
Chris Huss 18, 40-41, 56 (top left)

Norbert Wu 58, 79

INTRODUCTION

A hungry tiger shark polishes off another meal off the coast of Australia. Although mainly a fish eater, this is an aggressive species which should not be provoked by divers.

The mere glimpse of a triangular black fin slicing through the water is enough to arouse fear and panic in most onlookers. Because such a sight conjures up images of huge, gaping jaws and rows of sharp teeth, one's immediate reaction is to get away as far as possible and at great speed.

What is it about sharks that causes this feeling of terror? Are they all killers, intent on hunting down their victims—especially human ones—or is there more to the life of a shark than just hunting its prey?

In the minds of most people, the shark is a large, fast-swimming, ruthless predator that cruises the oceans in search of prey, particularly in the form of humans. The feared great white shark has done more to cloud people's opinions of sharks than any of the other species, most of which are harmless to humans. Well over 350 species of sharks are known to science, and they can be found in all the world's oceans, from the polar regions to the equator, and at all depths, from the surface and the seashore to the deepest ocean troughs. Some live in estuarine conditions, finding their way into river mouths, and one or two species are able to live in fresh water in large river systems. There is nowhere in the world's oceans, except perhaps for the most heavily polluted or over-fished regions, where sharks cannot be found. Given their abundance and sheer variety, sharks bear closer examination. As we begin to understand them better, we come to appreciate them more fully.

The excellent camouflage of the Pacific angel shark helps it blend with its background on a sandy seabed. The broad mouth is surrounded by sensory barbels, which detect food in the dark.

The white-tip reef shark is a common species around reefs and submerged rocks, easily recognised by its white fin tips. It is a fish eater, and is also curious about human swimmers but usually not aggressive.

THE FAMILY OF SHARKS

Most sharks are fish eaters and have powerful, streamlined bodies to help them swim quickly and catch their prey. Their eyes are usually quite adept at detecting movement and working in poor light conditions, while their teeth are sharp and point backwards to help capture and hold fast-moving, slippery prey. Some sharks feed on molluscs and crustaceans on the seabed; these have flatter teeth, capable of crushing the hard shells of crabs and clams. The curious cookie-cutter shark has a rounded mouth and sharp teeth, which enables it to take circular bites out of the skin of large whales, leaving round scars the shape of cookies. The largest predators, specialising in capturing other sharks or marine mammals like sea lions, possess big, triangular teeth with serrated edges. These shear over each other, whilst the giant yet harmless plankton feeders have no teeth at all. Such is the variety in this fascinating world.

Unusual Sharks

The most primitive of all the sharks so far discovered is the frilled shark. It is so named because of the frill-like appearance of its long gill flaps and is found mainly in the Pacific Ocean. It has a 2-metre- (6.5-foot-) long eel-like body and lives in very deep water, usually below 300 metres (990 feet), feeding on fish. Females give birth to about ten live young at a time.

The six- and seven-gilled sharks can easily be identified because they have more than the five gill slits normally found in all the other sharks. They are mostly confined to cold-water areas. When they occur in the tropical regions they live at great depths, where the water is coldest, and some have been found

Following page: The epaulette, or bamboo, shark is a small species found in shallow, warm waters, often near reefs, where its markings help it remain camouflaged.

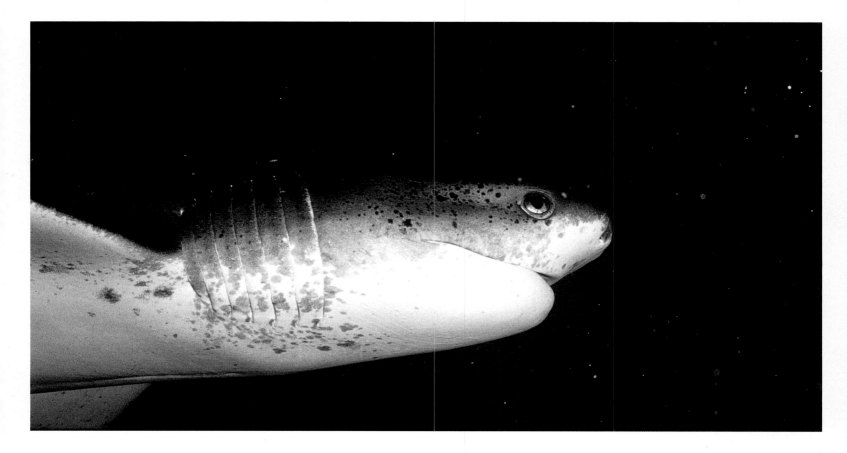

A school of scalloped hammerhead sharks swims in search of food in the Sea of Cortez, Mexico. These large concentrations are often made up of females only. There are several incidences of hammerheads attacking divers.

A seven-gilled blunt-nosed shark differs from most sharks in having seven gill slits; it prefers cold water, hence it usually lives in deeper water than other species, avoiding the warmer surface layers.

over 1,800 metres (5,940 feet) down. Near the poles, these sharks frequent shallow coastal waters. They can reach lengths of 4.5 metres (15 feet) and have long, tapering teeth in their upper jaws and short, serrated teeth in their lower jaws—ideal for preying on fish. The eggs develop inside the female, and about forty young are produced in each litter.

Bottom Dwellers

Horn sharks are bottom dwellers and are normally sluggish, inoffensive creatures, up to 1 metre (3.3 feet) long. They have two different types of teeth, pointed at the front and flattened at the back, which help them catch and then crush molluscs and crustaceans. This shark's common name refers to the prominent ridges above its eyes. The horn shark's attractive markings, small size, and diet of shellfish have made it a popular specimen in aquaria.

The orectoloboids comprise a large family (Orectolobidae), which spends a great deal of time actually resting on the seabed. Their pectoral fins are especially adapted to be used as 'feet' so that they can walk on them. Some actually do walk, rather than swim, away from danger if disturbed. In order to find shellfish (their favourite food), many employ sensory whiskerlike barbels around their

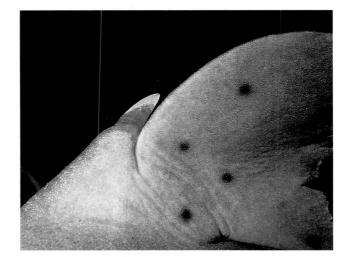

Used for defence, sharp spines are located just in front of the two dorsal fins of the horn shark. This small shark is often attacked as it searches for molluscs on the seabed.

The zebra horn shark is one of the more striking horn sharks, with vivid markings and very sharp dorsal spines. This small, colourful species is often collected for display at aquaria.

The horn sharks are best known for the sharp spines in front of the dorsal fins, used for defence. Their downward-pointing mouths are ideal for picking up sea urchins and molluscs.

The Port Jackson horn shark is well suited to life on the seabed. It has a large mouth for picking up shellfish and powerful back teeth for crushing shells. The horny ridges over the eyes—which inspired its name—show clearly here.

The spotted wobbe-
gong is a curious,
bottom-living shark
with excellent nat-
ural camouflage.
During the day
it remains hidden
and moves very
little, but at night
it becomes a little
more active as it
searches for food.

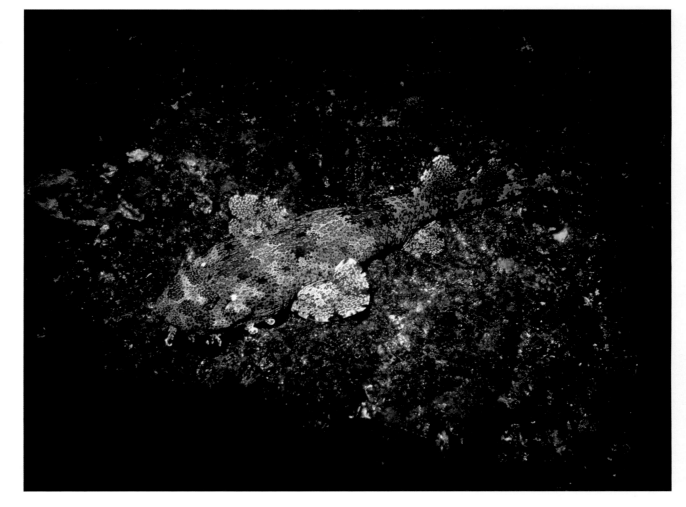

The ornate wobbe-
gong shark does
its best to look
like the coral- and
seaweed-covered
rocks where it
dwells. Small fish
come close to it
without realising
the danger and
are soon eaten.

The wobbegong shark has an extraordinary frilled appearance and beautiful mottled markings. It can easily hide amongst seaweeds, corals, and gravel on the seabed, lying in wait for smaller fish to come close.

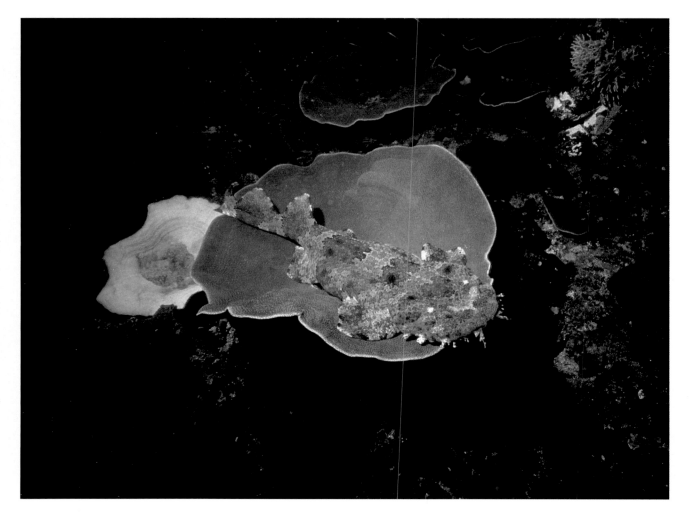

A small, ornate wobbegong shark rests on a coral in Coff's Harbour, New South Wales, Australia. When it chooses the correct background it can be almost impossible to see.

Just below the eye of this bamboo shark is an opening known as a spiracle, through which water passes on its way to the gills. Underneath the mouth are sensitive barbels, typical of species which feed on the seabed and in poor light conditions.

The huge whale shark may reach a length of 20 metres (66 feet), rivalling some of the true whales. Its under-surface is always white, with the green flanks attractively marked with spots.

mouths. This family includes the carpet sharks and nurse sharks, some of which eat bottom-living fish and have sharper teeth than the others.

The one exception to the rule in this family is the rare whale shark, the largest fish in the world, measuring up to 15 metres (49.5 feet) long. Found in the world's warmer waters, its huge body is greenish and covered with rows of large white dots. It has the same proportions as most other large sharks, except that it is far larger and has an enormous, flattened head and a vast, gaping, rectangular mouth devoid of teeth. The whale shark swims slowly near the surface of the water, sieving out the plankton. Very little is known about its habits or how it reproduces. At one time it was thought that it laid eggs in the form of giant 'mermaid's purses', but it is now believed that it produces live young, the eggs being retained inside the female until they have completed their development. A keen-eyed fish biologist once spotted a young whale shark on sale in a fish market in Oman, a country on the Arabian Sea. The shark was a perfect miniature version of the adult, but on the underside there was an umbilical scar, which suggested that it had been attached inside the female, rather than developing inside an egg. With such a rare species, a single incident like this is very valuable, but the data should be treated with caution. A large egg case attributed to the whale shark and measuring 68 by 40 centimetres (26.5 by 15.5 inches) was dredged from the seabed in the Gulf of Mexico, but this may have passed out of the female before development was complete.

The nurse shark is a nocturnal species which finds its food at night with the aid of sensory barbels around its mouth. Its eyes are much smaller than those of most other sharks.

Cat Sharks, Dogfish, Sand Tigers, and Other Species

The cat sharks and false cat sharks live in cold, deep waters in all the world's oceans, often frequenting the seabed to feed on shellfish. Most are small, rarely exceeding 1.5 metres (5 feet) in length, though the false cat shark can reach 3 metres (10 feet).

The swell sharks have an unusual defence mechanism, being able to take air or, more usually, water into their stomach and swell up to three or four times their normal size. A familiar member of this family is the lesser spotted dogfish, which as with many species of cat sharks, is quite palatable and is sold for human consumption. For example, in Britain its flesh masquerades under the name of 'rock salmon'.

Smooth dogfish sharks dwell in shallow waters, usually in warmer areas. Some may reach a length of 2 metres (6.5 feet). They swim over the seabed, rather than resting or crawling over it, and prey on molluscs, crustaceans, and flatfish. Most members of this family have strong migratory instincts, moving to temperate regions in the summer and returning to the tropics in the winter. Females support their embryos in the uterus, producing about ten young at a time.

Illuminated by a photographer's light, a brown-banded cat shark rests on the seabed. This small species prefers deep, cool water and feeds mostly on small fish and molluscs.

Another noteworthy type is the soup-fin shark. It is quite popular in the Orient, where its fins are the principal ingredient of shark-fin soup. Also well known, the eastern Pacific leopard shark is often seen in public aquaria, where onlookers admire its pleasing patterns of dark spots on a silvery background.

The sand tiger and goblin sharks are larger species, often growing to lengths of 3.5 metres (11.5 feet). The fish-eating sand tigers have long, thin teeth and look very fierce, but they actually have a fairly docile

Three white-tip reef sharks rest on the seabed amongst a colourful, mixed shoal of reef-dwelling fish. This is one of the smaller sharks, reaching a length of little more than 2 metres (6.5 feet).

A varied cat shark lies on the seabed amongst sea grasses off the coast of Victoria, Australia. When it finds shellfish and small fish after searching in the sand, this shark quickly consumes them with its powerful teeth, capable of crushing shells and spines.

A Caribbean reef shark rests in a colourful nook whilst a tiny Spanish hogfish hovers near its dorsal fin searching for skin parasites, which it removes and eats.

Grey reef sharks find most of their food close to the reef and spend much of their time cruising along near the bottom or along submerged cliff edges. They are curious about humans and will approach swimmers.

Should prey pass by a white-tip reef shark, it will doubtless be startled by a sudden attack. After the shark takes a quick bite or two, it will return to its resting place.

A large zebra shark glides past two underwater photographers in the Andaman Sea off the coast of Thailand. It normally remains camouflaged near the seabed.

The striking leopard, or zebra, shark is an unusual species sometimes found off the Great Barrier Reef in small numbers. It usually hunts amongst the coral, where its markings act as camouflage.

rest of the body. If the shark encounters a shoal of fish, it swims into the middle of it, threshing its tail around violently. This action usually stuns many fish and kills others, making them much easier to eat. These sharks can reach a length of over 6 metres (20 feet) and females give birth to live young, which may be as much as 1.5 metres (5 feet) long when newly born.

Megamouths

The bizarre megamouth was officially discovered in 1976 off the Hawaiian coast after it became accidentally entangled in an anchor cable and was given the name 'megamouth' on account of its enormous gape. The fish measured 4.5 metres (15 feet) in length and was the cause of much debate and argument amongst fish biologists. Several additional megamouths were caught after this, always as a result of entanglements; others washed ashore dead. Only in 1990 was a living specimen caught off California, and this was later returned to the sea alive.

The megamouth is now known to be a deepwater filter feeder, swimming through the murky depths straining water through its gills and extracting millions of tiny crustaceans. Unlike the other filter feeders, its mouth contains special light-emitting organs, possibly a means of attracting food in the dark ocean depths.

demeanour, so they are popular in public aquaria, where some have been in captivity for over twenty years. The false sand tiger shark lives in deep waters of the Indian and Atlantic oceans and has unusually large eyes. The goblin shark has an extraordinary appearance, with a long, thin flap of tissue sticking out from its forehead; the function of this feature is unknown, as is much of the rest of the biology of this species.

Threshers

Threshers have distinctive tails, unlike that of any other sharks. The upper lobe of the tail can be as long as the rest of the body and look almost whiplike in comparison with the

A Caribbean reef shark cruises amongst the corals in search of food. It prefers areas where it can find some cover in the coral and then make sudden attacks on its prey.

Mackerel Sharks

The mackerel sharks, of the family Lamnidae, include the notorious great white shark and many other large and occasionally dangerous species. One member, the mako shark, is possibly the fastest-swimming fish in the world, having been recorded at speeds of over 95 kilometres (58 miles) per hour; this enables it to overcome swordfish. Its fast speeds, exciting leaps out of the water, and tasty flesh make this a sought-after species amongst fishermen; as a result it is becoming scarce in some areas. The por-beagle and salmon sharks are the smallest members of this family, and they too are fast-swimming fish eaters. Females only give birth to one offspring at a time, producing several infertile eggs in the uterus for the single newborn to feed on.

Another type of mackerel shark, the basking shark, is the second-largest fish in the sea (the whale shark is largest). It is likely to be encountered in colder waters, often turning up in the summer off the coasts of Britain and northern Europe or in such plankton-rich areas of the Atlantic as the

The short-fin mako shark is one of the fastest-swimming sharks and uses its great speed to pursue other large open-water fish, such as tuna.

A diver is dwarfed by an approaching great white shark as he prepares to shoot with his camera. As long as the shark is not provoked by sudden movements or stimulated by the scent of blood the diver will be safe from attack.

Gulf of Maine. The basking shark cruises slowly along just below the surface with its snout projecting above the waves and its mouth gaping open below. Its triangular dorsal fin also breaks the surface, and the tip of the tail flops from side to side beyond it. When viewed from close quarters, the mouth appears white inside and the open gill slits behind the mouth reveal additional red gills.

In the warmer months of the year, when there is an abundance of plankton, the basking shark lives near the surface, often very close to the shore, but in the winter it is not seen. Very little is known about its habits during this time, but the findings of deep-sea fishermen indicate that it descends to the seabed in the colder months and enters a state of hibernation, remaining completely inactive until food is available again in the spring. This shark even appears to lose its gill rakers, as it will have no need for them until it starts filter-feeding again. The breeding habits of this species are also a mystery to scientists, as young, or egg-bearing, females are rarely seen. It is apparent that it is very slow to reproduce and is also becoming much more scarce, so it is one of the sharks which is in special need of protection. It is still fished for commercially around the northern European coastline on account of its enormous oil-rich liver, which occupies most of its body cavity. Returns from fishermen indicate that each year their catches are smaller and smaller, yet they still hunt it with harpoons, killing all they can find. In complete contrast, off some parts of the British coastline tourists are taken out to feeding areas in zodiacs and are able to watch this placid animal feeding and on some occasions actually touch it as it swims near them just below the surface.

The feared great white shark is one of the largest and most dangerous predators in the ocean. Even with the mouth partially opened, the fearsome teeth are clearly visible. This shark's name is not very accurate, as it is only white on the underside with a brown colouration above.

Requiem Sharks

The requiem sharks constitute a very large family (Carcharhinidae) of over one hundred species. Most of them have the typical shark shape and colouration. At over 6 metres (20 feet) in length, the largest is the tiger shark; it has the reputation for eating anything that will fit inside its mouth, from human beings to car tyres! It is also one of the most dangerous sharks ever encountered.

Also a member of the family, the bull shark, found all over the world, is one of the species which regularly enters fresh water. Indeed, it has been recorded over 1,000 kilometres (620 feet) from the sea in rivers such as the Mississippi and Zambesi. The hammerheads have bizarre protuberances on either side of their head which support their eyes; otherwise their bodies have conventional shark proportions. These projections probably have more to do with the detection of minute electrical impulses than improving vision. The great hammerhead, growing to a length of over 5 metres (16.5 feet), is one of the most aggressive species, and there are several records of attacks on humans.

The blue shark is a beautifully streamlined, fast-swimming shark of the open ocean. Its blue colouration helps camouflage it as it swims near the surface. Blue sharks are voracious predators which feed mainly at night.

A young tiger shark can be recognised by its striped flanks, but it also shows the broad head and prominent nostrils typical of this species. When mature it could reach a length of 7 metres (23 feet).

The scalloped
hammerhead has
a streamlined body
shape like most
other sharks and
is a fast swimmer,
but its strange
head is unique.
The eyes are locat-
ed at the ends
of the scalloped
head projections.

The streamlined
blue shark is
designed for speed
and perfectly suited
to the open ocean,
where it hunts
fast-swimming
fish. It sometimes
searches for them
beneath floating
rafts of seaweed.

The great hammer-
head shark is able
to locate its prey
by means of electri-
cal signals, which
it picks up with
special sensory
cells located on the
lateral head pro-
jections. Its teeth
are arranged in
several backward-
pointing rows.

The spiny dogfish shark lives in cold waters all around the world. It ranges in size from less than 30 centimetres (12 inches) to over 6 metres (20 feet). Many of them feed in deep water on squid. The spiny dogfish is the most common shark species in the north Atlantic Ocean, and many tonnes are caught each year for food. There is a venom-producing gland at the base of a sharp spine on the dorsal fins, which can produce a painful sting if handled carelessly. Many of the species which live in deeper water can produce light from special organs along the sides of their bodies. These probably attract squid, but may also act as a form of camouflage. They have large eyes, which work

When it settles on the seabed and flicks sand and gravel over its body, the Pacific angel shark is unnoticed by other predators and by its prey. Tiny fish and crabs are easily attacked if they come within range.

One of the most common of all the small sharks is the spiny dogfish, or spur-dog, found in shoals of thousands in the north Atlantic and North Sea. Venomous spines are located in front of the dorsal fins.

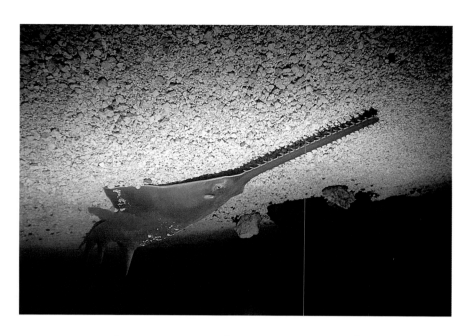

A Pacific angel shark has a strange, flattened body with enlarged pectoral fins, which give it the appearance of wings. It spends most of its time near the seabed lying in wait for food.

The sawfish uses its rostrum to stir up the seabed and uncover food. The fish also uses this dual-purpose appendage to thrash through shoals of fish, killing its dinner in the process.

well in very low light levels. The strange sleeper sharks, which live permanently in the cold waters of the Arctic, are sometimes found beneath the ice caps. They are fish eaters but will also prey on seals, and they are unusual in having flesh which is poisonous to humans and dogs. Bramble sharks have widely spaced dermal denticles on their skin, giving them a prickly, 'brambly' appearance.

The angel sharks are flattened and look more like the skates and rays. They can grow up to 2 metres (6.5 feet) long and live in shallow water, waiting for prey to pass close by. For much of the time they are sluggish and lethargic, but when prey is near or if they are hooked by an angler, these sharks are transformed into far more lively fish. They have very powerful jaws and are reluctant to let go of anything they capture, including the hand of an angler trying to remove a hook.

The saw sharks have a long snout, or rostrum, with a serrated edge, resembling that of a sawfish. They are not often seen, spending most of their time near the seabed in search of shellfish. Their teeth are used for crushing their food, the 'saw' functioning principally as a defence against predators.

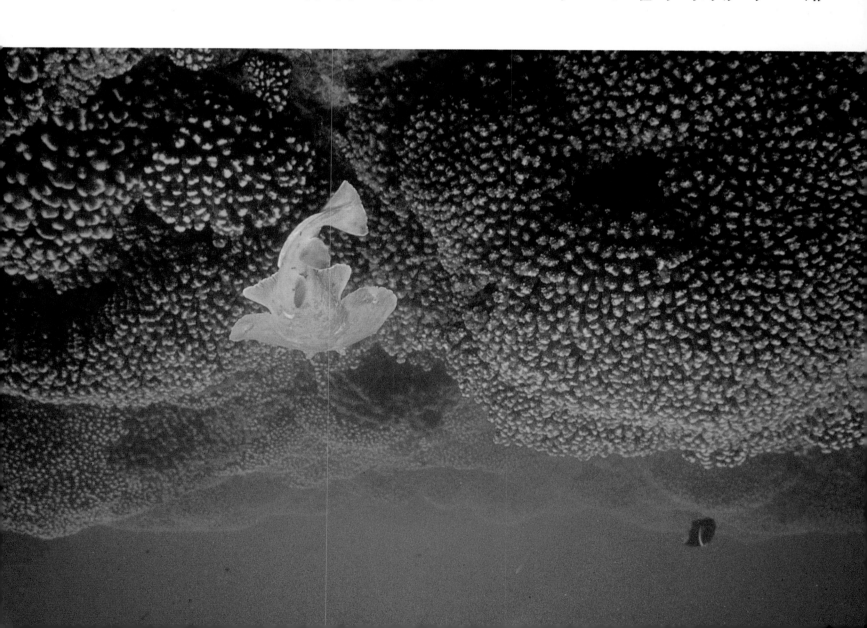

Skates, Rays, and Chimaeras

Skates and rays are close relatives of the sharks—differing principally in that they have flattened bodies. In many respects they are very similar, having a cartilaginous skeleton, a skin covered with dermal denticles, five gill slits, and a similar method of reproduction. With a few exceptions, most of them live on the seabed, acting as scavengers or feeding on molluscs, crustaceans, and flatfish. Most species are edible and many are fished commercially. Their nearest shark relatives are the angel sharks and saw sharks. Their bodies are flattened from top to bottom, with strong projections on either side; these 'wings' are used with great effect for swimming. The gill slits are on the underside and water enters the body through two large spiracles, or vents, on top of the head near the eyes.

A type of ray, the sawfish is easy to identify, as it has a strong sawlike snout, which it uses for a variety of purposes: to kill or injure fish, to dig for shellfish, and to defend itself.

The electric ray family can produce strong electric currents. Most live in shallow water, swimming slowly over the seabed and using electric shocks to stun their prey. The organs which produce the electricity are located at the base of their pectoral fins, and they can emit shocks of up to 300 volts at a time.

There are about 120 species in the skate family, Rajidae, and they are

The eye of a skate displays its fimbriated iris, which retracts like a window blind. The eyes of this bottom-dwelling fish lie on top of the head, and the spiracle is located immediately behind it.

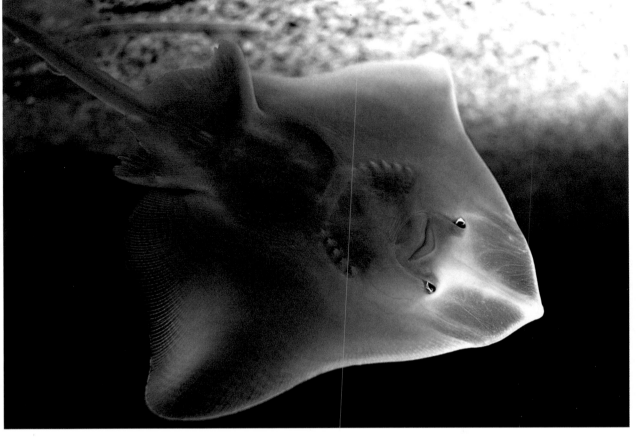

The underside of the big skate, normally lying flat on the seabed, reveals the crescent-shaped mouth, ideal for picking up shellfish from the seabed, and the rows of gill slits, typical of other shark species.

A southern stingray glides over a reef. When it settles to rest in shallow water, this ray can be a hazard to divers who may step on it and receive a painful sting.

The Pacific manta ray is one of the largest of all the rays, but its prey is composed of tiny planktonic creatures, which it catches in its large mouth.

Spotted eagle rays appear to fly through the water, using their 'wings' to swim. They often swim in small schools, preferring shallow water with a sandy seabed.

*The strikingly attractive spotted eagle ray
uses its snout to grub through the sand
in search of molluscs and crustaceans.*

found in cool waters all around the world. They nearly always live on the seabed feeding on molluscs and crustaceans. The little skate, found off the Atlantic coast of North America, is the smallest—measuring only 50 centimetres (19.5 inches) long and weighing 450 grams (barely 1 pound)—whilst the big skate, from the Pacific coast, grows to over 2.5 metres (8.2 feet) long and may weigh in at 90 kilograms (198 pounds). Members of this family have pointed snouts and diamond-shaped bodies. Females lay their eggs in tough, leathery egg cases, often found washed up on beaches after storms and commonly known as mermaid's purses. Some species have specially modified pelvic fins, enabling them to 'walk' over the seabed. Their tails are usually long, whiplike, and armed with spines for defence; many species have electric organs capable of producing a four-volt shock, possibly used in courtship.

A pair of remoras, or cling fish, is attached to the head of a manta ray; specially adapted pectoral fins act as suckers to help them adhere to the larger fish.

A pelagic stingray is pursuing a school of mating squid off the California coast at night. Normally confined to the seabed, the stingray will move nearer the surface when darkness falls.

Stingrays have venom-producing glands on their spiny tails; exposure to these can produce a very painful sting, which is usually not fatal. The barbed, needle-shaped spines penetrate the skin easily but prove very difficult to remove. The Atlantic stingray is a mere 30 centimetres (12 inches) across, but the Indo-Pacific stingray is over 2 metres (6.5 feet) wide, measured across the disc-shaped body, and 4.5 metres (15 feet) long. It lives in shallow water. On the Australian coast, it has been known to thrust its spines into the chests of unwary swimmers, usually with fatal results. Some species can live in fresh water and in the large river systems of South America, where they are feared by the native Indians.

Eagle rays have large wings and often are beautifully marked with coloured spots on contrasting backgrounds. They have a snub-nosed appearance and a rounded shape. They can often be found in large shoals, sometimes leaping out of the water and gliding for short distances. Eagle rays make small excavations in the sand in search of buried shellfish.

The giants of this family are the manta rays, which can have a wingspan of over 6 metres

The bow-mouth guitarfish has a flattened, raylike body, but it resembles that of a shark. Its large mouth is filled with strange, flattened teeth for crushing shells.

The chimaera, or ratfish, is a deep-water species of the coldest regions. Because it is a very poor swimmer, it spends much of its time sitting motionlessly on the seabed. This forbidding fish has a sharp spine with a venom sac at its base.

(20 feet) and weigh more than 1,600 kilograms (3,527 pounds). Although vast in size, they are not dangerous predators, but peaceful plankton feeders. Mantas often swim in small schools and occasionally make spectacular leaps into the air. The sight of these huge black-and-white fish with their large wings and whiplike tail flying clear of the water is one of the most memorable to be seen in the open ocean.

There are reports of females giving birth to their young as they leap, but there is no clear reason as to why they regularly do this. The young develop inside the mother, nourished by a fluid known as 'uterine milk'. The leaping mantas could be attempting to dislodge parasites from their bodies, or the breaching could also be a form of display or communication. Whatever the reason, it is a sight not to be missed. Manta rays are not interested in fishermen's bait, and are generally too fast to be caught by netting or spearing, so this species is not in any immediate danger, but is vulnerable to entanglements.

The chimaeras are very strange fish to look at—not resembling sharks, rays, or any other members of this family. They have many similarities internally, but externally look more like gurnards. The name derives from a story in Greek mythology about a she-monster with the body of a goat, the head of a lion, and the tail of a snake. They live at great depths in cold waters near the polar regions and are not often seen, except by fishermen using deepwater trawl nets.

The blue-spotted stingray is one of the most attractive of the bottom-living rays. It is also known as the ribbon-tail ray and often lies in shallow water over reefs.

THE SHARK AS PREDATOR

Only about thirty shark species are large and aggressive enough to attack humans, and of those only a few have been known to do so on a regular basis. The great white is notorious for its attacks on swimmers, but the hammerhead, the bull, the mako, and the tiger sharks all make attacks under certain circumstances.

The oceanic white-tip, the black-tip, and the grey nurse sharks also make attacks, although the actual number of incidents each year is very small. These sharks are often described as 'man eaters', but this is not strictly true, as they usually find human flesh unpalatable and eat very little of their victims. This is a rather academic point, however, as whether or not a person is eaten makes very little difference in the outcome of an attack on a defenceless swimmer by a voracious shark.

When there is a shark attack it makes the headlines and arouses various emotions. The shark is invariably portrayed as a vicious killer deliberately seeking human

A blue shark approaches a sea lion in the open sea. The sea lion is probably safe here, as it is not injured and has plenty of room to escape, but it could become prey if it were sick or unable to swim quickly away.

A mackerel makes a tasty snack for a hungry blue shark and comprises one of the principal parts of its diet. Usually, shoals of mackerel attract many ravenous sharks, and although the mackerel is a fast swimmer, it cannot escape the powerful jaws of the speedy blue shark.

prey. Long-term studies of shark attacks have shown that they are usually the result of people venturing into the shark's habitat and in some cases provoking an attack by swimming too close or making sudden, startling movements. Far more people die in road traffic accidents on their way to the beach on a normal holiday weekend than ever get killed by sharks.

Water Temperature

Statistics show that most shark attacks occur in water with temperatures above 21 degrees C (70 degrees F). This would seem to indicate that temperature is a critical factor in attacks, and if the water is below this temperature it is safe to swim even if sharks are present. However, it should be remembered that most people prefer to swim when the water is warmer, and below 21 degrees C the water is not as inviting to the less hardy swimmers. Could it be that the greater numbers of bathers in the warmer water triggers

A fishy bait attracts a great white shark toward a diver protected inside a shark cage. The diver must not stick his arm out of the cage or he would be in great danger of attack.

A great white shark attacks bait designed to attract it toward a safety cage. The lips have rolled back, exposing the rows of teeth. This is an indication that the shark is ready to bite.

aggressive behaviour rather than the rise in temperature? Is it the abundance of potential victims on warm days that initiates attacks on swimmers? A sudden rise in temperature coinciding with a holiday weekend—resulting in large numbers of people flocking to the beach—may be just the stimulus required to provoke an attack.

Water Depth

Attacks can take place in any depth of water where the shark can swim. They can occur on the shore where people are paddling along the very edge of the sea, in shallow lagoons amongst mangroves, or in the open ocean after a capsizing incident. Those attacks which happen in the open ocean are more often likely to end in death, as the victims are completely at the mercy of the animals and are a long way from help.

Sharks are often seen swimming very close to the shore in water only just deep enough to cover them, and some have been known to lunge at the feet of paddlers and strand themselves as the waves recede; some even appear to be following the movements of people walking along the shore just beyond the waves. Many cruise along submerged

The rows of triangular teeth in the mouth of this great white shark are continually being replaced; as the front teeth wear out, new teeth are ready to grow in from behind. Each tooth has a sawtooth edge to give it greater cutting power.

The strange silhouette of the scalloped hammerhead shark stands out clearly amongst the shoal of small creole fish. It will feed on these fish, but also attacks larger marine mammals and human divers. The hammerheads have smaller pectoral fins than other large sharks.

cliffs, following regular routes in search of prey. Hammerheads can often be seen on the edges of reefs, sometimes in large numbers, swimming rapidly along the reef edge in search of prey.

Hunt Behaviour

Most of the large sharks hunt alone, relying on their own senses to locate prey. If they find something and start to feed on it, the commotion, or the release of blood into the water, will soon attract other sharks if they are within 1 kilometre (.6 mile) of the kill. As they home in on the food and start their own attacks, a feeding frenzy will follow, the water boiling with the threshing bodies of excited sharks. This is what is usually seen by human observers, giving the impression that the sharks have made the kill together. Some of the smaller species of sharks do hunt together, usually in search of such small prey as crabs and bottom-living fish.

The sand tiger shark is found in shallow water in the warmer parts of the world and has a reputation as a killer in some areas. It is best avoided by divers and should not be approached. Its menacing appearance is usually enough to keep people away.

A great white shark breaks the surface and attacks a mannequin dressed in a diver's wet suit. Real divers are often attacked, probably having been mistaken for sea lions, which are this shark's natural prey. This experiment, conducted by the Steinhart Aquarium in San Francisco, showed that sharks will attack prey on the surface; the mannequin was torn to pieces.

A juvenile lemon shark finds safety from the attacks of other sharks in a shallow lagoon amongst the mangroves of the Bahamian coast.

The tasselled wobbegong shark has a huge, broad mouth, which makes it easy for it to suddenly swallow an unsuspecting fish. This species was thought to be harmless to humans until someone acciden- tally stepped on one and received a painful bite.

Prey Detection

Like all other large predators, the shark has an efficient sensory system to help it locate its prey. It can detect blood and the scent of other body fluids from a distance of about 1 kilometre (.6 mile). It can follow the scent trail upstream accurately and then use its other senses as it gets within 150 metres (165 yards) to pinpoint the prey. Its sensory pits and lateral line easily pick up the disturbances made by movement in the water, and it is particularly sensitive to unnatural sounds and movements, such as those made by an injured animal.

Sharks use their eyes when they are within about 25 metres (27 yards) of prey, even in poor light conditions. In this way, they can accurately use their jaws to make the final capture. A further set of sensory structures—which can detect the minute electrical currents generated by the nervous systems of other living things—takes over when the shark is only a short distance away. The more the prey struggles and thrashes around in the water, the greater the electrical stimulation detected by the shark.

The Kill

The shark's bite is very powerful, especially that of large species like the great white, but

A bull shark, accompanied by remoras and pilot fish, swims in shallow water; it often enters fresh water and swims for great distances up large rivers like the Mississippi and Zambesi. This is a dangerous species, especially if encountered in confined waters.

Blue sharks sometimes feed on tiny shrimp known as krill. They typically swim around large groups of them several times, causing the shrimp to move together. This enables the shark to gulp down large mouthfuls at a time.

most of the damage is done as the rows of sharp, backward-pointing, triangular teeth shear over each other. As well as biting and gripping its prey, the shark also shakes it around in the water, and this is how large chunks of flesh can be removed. With very large prey, a shark tends to grip tightly and then twist around until a large piece of flesh has been removed. Just before the first bite,

the lips of the great white shark roll back and the snout rises to fully expose the fearsome array of teeth. It pushes its jaw forward, enabling it to bite directly in front rather than from the side. The jaws of large sharks snap shut when they make contact with a solid object—a reflex action that takes place even if the shark's mouth hits inanimate objects like fishing floats or surfboards. This explains why

such a curious array of objects—ranging from fishing tackle and plastic debris to car headlamps and glass bottles—has been found inside the stomachs of dead sharks. It is unlikely that sharks would have sought these items as food, but they may well have come in contact with them while swimming through shipping lanes where man-made objects are regularly thrown overboard.

Some shark attacks are totally unexpected, preceded by a quiet approach. A shark might even appear to be about to swim past the victim, unaware of its presence. It will then suddenly grab the prey, shake it around for a short time, and swim off, but not without leaving severe wounds. A more violent form of attack involves the shark making repeated, frenzied strikes, resulting in numerous severe and almost always fatal wounds.

If one grey reef shark finds food, others are sure to join in, producing a feeding frenzy. During these communal meals, sharks will often attack their own kind, making smaller sharks especially vulnerable.

ANATOMY OF A SHARK

The shark is a complex collection of senses, each perfectly synchronised with the others. Additionally, the shark's streamlined shape and powerful muscles make it a capable swimmer and formidable opponent.

Sight

Sharks have a curiously expressionless pair of eyes; to some people they look cold and menacing, whilst to others the rather small, unblinking sunken eyes convey no feeling at all. The shark's eyesight is probably about ten times more sensitive than that of humans in dim light, so it is well suited to locating prey, and each other, in murky water or at night. The eyes are protected by a nictitating membrane which slides across immediately before an attack, and in some species the eyes can roll back into the head for further protection from damage by the prey in its death throes.

The retina, or light-sensitive layer at the back of the shark's eye, consists of cells known as rods which are sensitive to movement and the contrast between light and dark. They do not have the ability to detect colour and are also unable to detect the shape or form of objects very accurately. Behind the retina is layer of crystals that reflects light back onto the retina, helping the light-sensitive cells to function at very low light levels. This layer gives the ghostly red-eye effect sometimes seen when a flash is used to take photographs. It seems that the shark's eyes are best suited to detecting movements of objects reasonably close to the shark and helping it to find prey in murky water.

The small opening next to the eye of this leopard shark is the spiracle through which water enters before passing over the gills.

The elegant, streamlined shape of the silky shark, seen in the Bahamas, displays a crescent-shaped mouth and large pectoral fins—essential for moving swiftly through the water when pursuing prey.

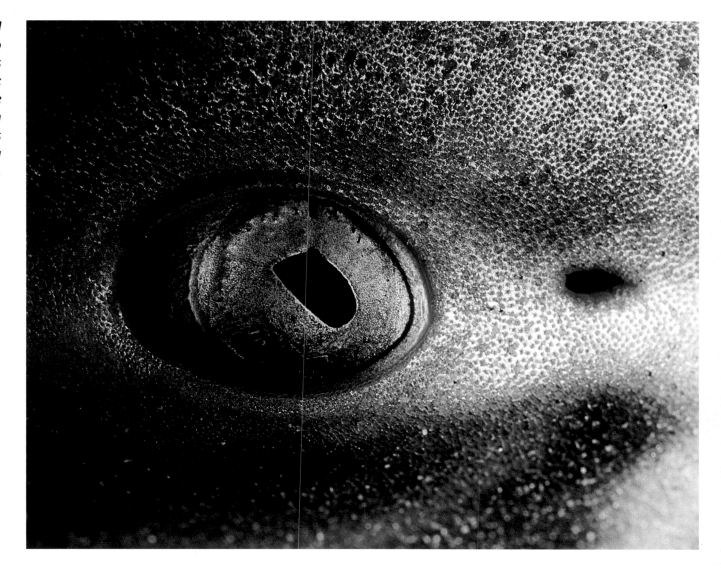

The long fins, pointed snout, and slender shape of this silky shark are designed for speed and skilful management when pursuing fast-swimming fish in the open ocean.

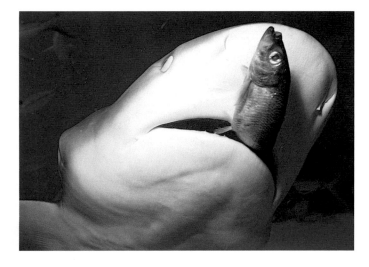

Though the mouth is located on the underside of the head away from the eyes, this area of the snout contains sensory organs for the detection of smell and movement, enabling the shark to locate and capture its prey.

A great white shark lunges at a fish bait off the Australian coast. At the moment of attack, the jaws open wide and the lips roll back to expose rows of huge teeth.

Sensory Pits

Around the snout of the shark are numerous tiny, jelly-filled pits, called the ampullae of Lorenzini, which resemble pinholes. Nerve endings in these pits are linked to the brain, and they are sensitive to minute electrical currents in the water. When living creatures make muscular movements, the electrical messages from their brains which control these movements can be detected by sharks nearby. This sense helps the shark to locate flatfish, which lie on the seabed in near darkness partly covered by sediment. The frantic movements of an injured prey animal will produce plenty of electrical activity to help guide the shark in for the kill. Boat owners and divers are sometimes startled to find a great white nuzzling up to their outboard motor or metal shark cage; these metallic objects often produce tiny electrical currents which must resemble those produced by the nervous systems of living creatures. The shark gets no response from inanimate objects like these and may make more and more frenzied attacks until driven away or if it becomes exhausted. Even if tempted with a smelly bait which would normally attract them, they will ignore this and carry on attacking the metal object.

Scalloped hammerheads swimming off the coast of Costa Rica will typically spend some time hunting fish near the surface. However, they can also descend to great depths in order to catch fish near the seabed, using their ability to detect electrical currents to locate prey in the dark.

The underside of the snout of this deep-sea cat shark, caught in the Pacific Ocean off the Galápagos Islands, shows the pits of the ampullae of Lorenzini, which are the site of the electrical sensors used by sharks to locate other living creatures.

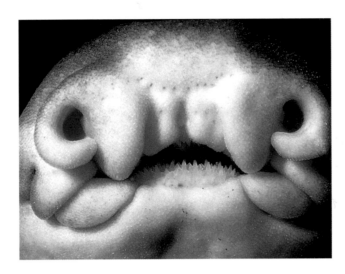

The horn shark displays rows of incisors for grasping prey and tiny pits housing its electrical sensors, used to detect the presence of living creatures.

The strange mouth of the tawny nurse shark is surrounded by sensitive barbels, enabling it to locate its food in murky water or at night. The nostrils near the mouth draw in water, which passes over special cells linked to the olfactory lobes of the brain.

Smell

Almost two-thirds of the shark's brain is devoted to the sense of smell. As it swims through the water, a shark draws a small current of sea water through the nostrils on either side of the snout. The side-to-side movement of the head makes it easier to pick up tiny traces of chemicals scattered in the water. Water forced into the nostrils passes over some sensory cells, which are able to detect chemicals in the water. These olfactory cells are linked by nerves to the olfactory lobes in the brain, which interpret the messages received. This part of the brain, which deals with the sense of smell, is far larger in sharks than other fish and far better developed than in most other vertebrates.

A shark can detect minute amounts of a chemical and finds blood and body fluids of greatest interest. The ability to detect scents from a great distance becomes more acute in sharks which have not found food for some time—and makes them far more dangerous if they are a large and aggressive species.

Heat Conservation

Sharks are described as 'cold-blooded' creatures, but this is a rather misleading term. Unlike mammals and birds, they do not have a constant body temperature; rather, it is similar to that of their surroundings. Unlike the marine mammals, which have a thick skin and a blubber layer beneath that, sharks have no means of conserving the heat produced by their tissues. However, some species are able to maintain their muscular tissue at a higher temperature than the water they are swimming in by having blood vessels arranged rather like heat exchangers. The vessels bring fresh, oxygen-bearing blood to the muscles and pass close by other vessels carrying carbon dioxide away. In the process, heat can pass from one to another rather than being dissipated around the body and lost through the skin. Warm muscles are more efficient than cold ones, and so a shark gains valuable time when making an attack if its muscles are warm and ready for action.

Hearing

Sharks do not produce any sounds themselves, but they do use sounds to locate potential prey. Certain sounds, such as the low-frequency vibrations produced as an animal struggles in the water, seem to be of great interest to some of the larger predatory sharks. Sounds which are near the lower limit of human hearing are the most likely to attract sharks. Experiments in which sounds in the range of 25 to 50 Hz were produced in shark-infested waters showed that they were

Having such small eyes is no problem to the nurse shark when searching for food, as it has highly sensitive barbels on either side of the mouth. These allow it to find its food in darkness.

Rows of sharp teeth line the mouth of the leopard shark, enabling it to get a good grip on fish. The dermal denticles, or toothlike skin scales, also show clearly around the mouth.

easily attracted. It has also been suggested that the dull, thudding sounds made by helicopter rotor blades attract sharks; this could be very dangerous if swimmers in distress were being rescued by a helicopter from shark-infested waters. The sounds made by a single person swimming in the open water often attract sharks from a great distance. The sensory cells which detect these sounds, which travel through the water in the form of pressure waves, are located in the fluid-filled canals of the lateral line. This important sense organ runs along either side of the body and is visible as a line of tiny pits. If vibrations hit one side of the body only, as they will do if the prey is off to one side, the shark knows to turn in the direction of the strongest stimulus and swim toward it. As it gets nearer, other stimuli, such as sight or electrical activity, may take over and guide it in for the kill.

Skin

The shark's skin feels rough to the touch. In some of the larger species, it has the texture of coarse sandpaper and has even been used as sandpaper when dried. Indeed, a large

shark thrashing about on the deck of a boat can inflict painful grazes on unprotected human skin if the tail rubs across it.

This roughness is due to the covering of thousands of tiny toothlike structures that project from the skin. These are the dermal denticles, which are quite different from the smooth, flattened scales found in the bony fish. They are all directed backward, to cut down on resistance to the flow of water and help in streamlining. The skin secretes a slimy mucus and this is trapped by the denticles, producing a sleek body covering which does not impede the flow of water.

Teeth

The shark's teeth are its most feared weapons. No other fish has such a formidable armoury. Row after row of sharp, triangular teeth is the sinister image many people have in their minds of all sharks, even the species like the basking shark, which do not possess any teeth at all. The large hunters, such as the great white and the tiger sharks, have large, triangular teeth with serrated edges for extra grip and power, but some of the smaller species have more pointed, and sometimes curved, teeth. In nearly all species the teeth point backward, making it impossible for a victim to escape from the mouth.

The teeth grow in rows on both jaws and they are continually being replaced from behind, so there are always new teeth ready for those which are worn or damaged. The jaws of the larger sharks are immensely powerful and combine with the rows of sharp teeth to give it its fearsome bite. Large sharks can slice through the thick shells of fully grown sea turtles and crocodiles, and they can make very quick work of human limbs. The jaws are not able to make chewing movements, as in grazing mammals, for example, but they are very powerful

The sand tiger, or grey nurse shark, is one of the group of 'ragged-toothed sharks' noted for their fanglike teeth. These help them catch and eat slippery fish, but can also inflict terrible wounds on other larger prey. Needless to say, this shark should not be provoked.

when opening and shutting. The teeth overlap slightly to produce a strong shearing action.

The mouth is normally on the underside of the head, below the snout, but the head and neck are flexible, so the snout can be tilted back and the jaws opened wide to allow the shark to take huge bites out of its victims. Photographs of the torsos of swimmers who have survived shark attacks show how large the jaws are; measuring the long, curved scars on such a person's chest can give the 'bite radius' of a shark. With a few bites of its large jaws, a great white or tiger shark can make short work of prey—even animals as large as a sea lion.

A school of rainbow runners mobs a silky shark, rubbing their flanks against its rough skin, possibly trying to rid themselves of fish lice attached to their bodies.

A tawny nurse shark feeds on a dead turtle floating near the surface. Carrion feeders often have a very good sense of smell to help them locate their food.

INDEX

*Page numbers in **bold-face** type indicate photo captions.*

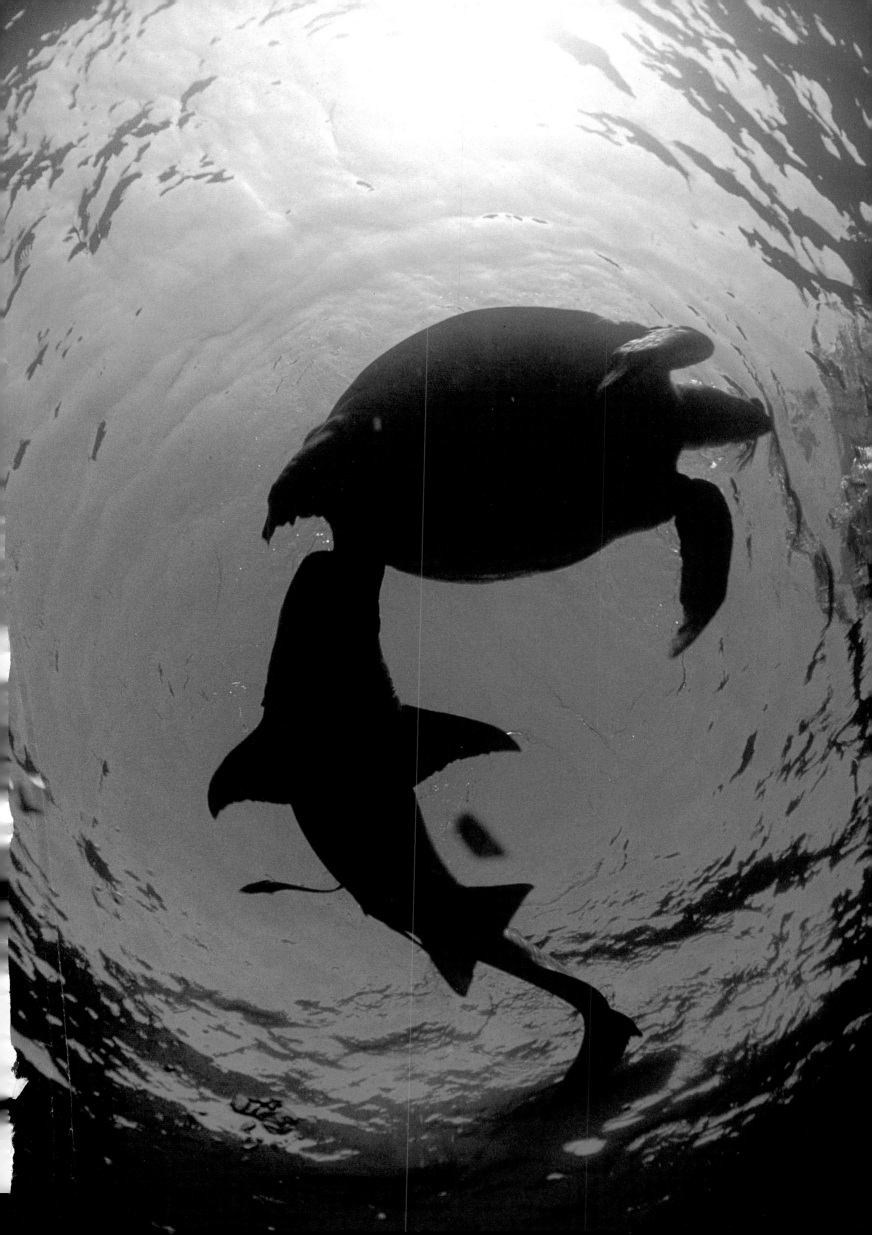

THE SHARK'S LIFE CYCLE

Though much of the shark's life habits remain a mystery, the subject is indeed a fascinating one. Many people are unaware that the shark actually has a courtship ritual and can give birth to live young—traits normally associated with animals that we do not find quite so formidable.

Courting and Reproduction

Male and female sharks of the same species look almost identical. The only visible difference is the presence of two large structures called 'claspers', which are really modified fins, on the underside of the male. These are important in the mating process and are used to guide the milt, or sperm, inside the female.

In most fish, fertilisation of the eggs is a random process, taking place in the water after eggs and sperm have been released by the female and male, sometimes in a frenzy of mass-spawning. In the sharks it is a much more controlled affair, and there is more certainty of the eggs being successfully fertilised.

Shark observers have occasionally witnessed courtship rituals. In some cases, the male makes advances to the female and twines his body around hers, but in many species the act of mating has never been observed by humans. Once the eggs have been fertilised they remain inside the female for a short time as the yolk sac and egg case develop.

Sharks produce large eggs in relatively small numbers, unlike smaller fish such as herring, which produce tiny eggs in tens of thousands. Each egg is provided with a large

A pair of nurse sharks twist their bodies around each other during courtship, immediately prior to mating. Unlike many other fish, sharks have internal fertilisation of the eggs.

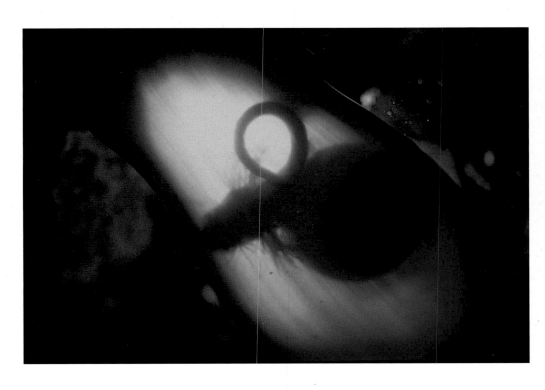

The projecting horns on the head of the manta ray impart a threatening appearance and inspired its other name of 'devil fish'. In reality, it is only a harmless plankton feeder.

The tiny embryo of a swell shark can be seen attached to the yolk sac inside its protective egg case. The small shark will remain inside the egg case for several months before its development is complete.

A tiny swell shark cautiously emerges from its protective egg case after completing several months of development.

The case is then anchored to the seabed by tendrils, keeping the small shark secure until it is able to swim free and fend for itself.

yolk sac to nourish the developing embryo and is usually protected inside a tough, leathery case. The chances of individual eggs hatching are high so the shark does not need to produce so many in order to ensure its survival. In some species the eggs are laid in cases in the shape of the familiar 'mermaid's purse', which so often wash up on the shore after storms. These are usually empty and dried up, but sometimes one is found with a tiny fish still living inside it.

The dogfish family, amongst the smallest of the sharks, produce eggs in this way, and many of the skates and rays lay large, flattened, and rather dark egg cases. A female dogfish typically lays about twenty eggs, and they take around eight to nine months to develop. When first laid by the female they are semitransparent and armed with long tendrils at each corner to anchor them securely on the seabed. The leathery skin is semitransparent and the yolk sac with the wriggling embryo attached is visible through the skin.

As the embryo develops, the yolk sac decreases in size and the embryo grows larger, and at the same time the outer skin of the egg case becomes opaque. When the development is complete the tiny dogfish, a perfect replica of the adult, wriggles out of

The small swell shark must search for its own food immediately after hatching, as the parents play no part in its upbringing and offer it no protection.

The lemon shark gives birth to live young, which are perfectly formed when they emerge from the womb.

the case and swims free. It may still have a little of the yolk sac attached to it, but this is soon absorbed. The tiny shark must then fend for itself. The chances are that many of the little ones will be eaten straight away by larger sharks and other fish, but enough will survive to produce another generation.

Many species of sharks give birth to live young. Instead of releasing the eggs and leaving them to develop attached to the seabed, they remain inside the female for extra protection and the young are released when fully developed.

There are two main ways in which this happens. In the ovoviviparous species, the eggs remain inside their cases in the womb, feeding off the yolk's food supply, and the eggs hatch internally before the young swim free. In the viviparous species, the embryo grows inside the womb attached to its wall by a yolk 'placenta', similar in some ways to the placenta of mammals. The gestation period varies in length depending on the species, but always takes several months. For some species, such as the giant basking shark and whale shark, virtually nothing is known about their breeding biology apart from a few chance observations.

A young lemon shark is able to swim immediately. Once it swims free, the newborn must fend for itself and find its own food.

A male white-tip reef shark turns to reveal the 'claspers' on the underside adjacent to the pectoral fins, which are used during mating.

Following page:
As with all plankton feeders, the whale shark has an enormous but toothless mouth to enable it to take in sea water. The diver in the background is dwarfed by this large fish.

Pilot and Cling Fish

Many sharks are accompanied by pilot fish, but these companions do not do what their name suggests. Instead these small fish, which swim perilously close to large sharks, are simply following, waiting for scraps of food to float by when the larger animal feeds. If they were not quick and agile swimmers they would get eaten themselves. Pilot fish probably gain some protection from other predatory fish by swimming near the shark.

As a lemon shark rests among sea grasses, a remora attaches itself to its head. It will not be attacked by the shark and is also safe here from the attacks of other fish.

The remoras, or cling fish, have taken this relationship one step further, and actually cling to the body of the shark with the aid of suckerlike structures on the tops of their bodies. They feed on scraps of food and also rid the shark's skin of external parasites. Numerous fish lice and other troublesome invertebrates attempt to attach themselves to the rough skin of the shark and make its body less hydrodynamic, so the cling fish are actually performing a useful service by keeping the skin clear of them. The slow-moving sharks like the whale shark often have several cling fish attached to them as they are more prone to external parasites. Very fast swimmers like the mako shark are less likely to have hangers-on.

An oceanic white-tip shark, easily recognised by its white fin tips, glides effortlessly along accompanied by a small school of pilot fish awaiting food scraps. This is one of the most common sharks of the open ocean and can grow to a length of 3.5 metres (16.5 feet).

Cloudy waters are usually rich in plankton, the food of the basking shark. It can be found off the coasts of Europe and frequents shallow water.

The enormous, gaping mouth of the basking shark, the second-largest fish in the sea, enables it to take in great volumes of plankton-rich sea water.

The huge meg-
amouth shark
is a recent discov-
ery and is very
rarely seen alive.
It inhabits deep
water, where it
feeds on plankton
and tiny shrimp,
and has special
light-emitting cells
around its mouth.

A school of small
cleaner fish clusters
around the tooth-
less mouth of the
whale shark as
it swims slowly
near the surface.

Afterword

For various reasons, some people see sharks as threats, and to them the only good shark is a dead one. This attitude has been responsible for the demise of the great white shark off the coast of Australia, where it is becoming increasingly scarce due to relentless persecution and so-called sport fishing. Blue sharks, porbeagles, and tope are hunted off the European coast and are also declining. Harmless and inoffensive species also suffer because of the reputation of the fiercer fish, and in many areas sharks are now becoming more difficult to find. Undoubtedly some sharks are a threat to human swimmers in the water, but most others are not. We know a great deal more about the behaviour of these magnificent fish and the important role they play in the ecology of the oceans. To simply wipe out entire species would be very foolish and could lead to unforeseen changes in the fish and invertebrate populations of parts of the oceans. It would be far better if we could learn to live with the sharks, accept them for what they are, and enjoy watching them in their natural environment. They have been on this planet far longer than we have and most certainly have an equal right to be here.

As the manta ray glides through the upper reaches of the ocean, large volumes of sea water pass through its large mouth and over its gill rakers, seen here at the back of the mouth. These filter out the plankton for consumption.

A whale shark, the largest fish in the sea, swims off the coast of the Seychelles. Despite its huge bulk, it feeds only on tiny planktonic creatures.